MW00916480

Behind the Desk With...

Matt Christopher®

The #1 Sportswriter for Kids

by Dale Christopher

LITTLE, BROWN AND COMPANY

New York ・ Boston

Little, Brown and Company

Time Warner Book Group
1271 Avenue of the Americas, New York, NY 10020
Visit our Web site at www.lb-kids.com

www.mattchristopher.com

First Edition

Matt Christopher® is a registered trademark of Catherine M. Christopher.

Library of Congress Cataloging-in-Publication Data

Christopher, Dale, 1947–
    Behind the desk with . . . Matt Christopher: the #1 sportswriter for
kids / by Dale Christopher. — 1st ed.
        p. cm.
    ISBN: 0-316-10952-5
    1. Christopher, Matt — Juvenile literature. 2. Sportswriters —
United States — Biography — Juvenile literature. 3. Authors,
American — 20th century — Biography — Juvenile literature.
4. Children's literature, American — Authorship — Juvenile
literature. [1. Christopher, Matt. 2. Authors, American.] I. Title.

GV742.42.C48C48 2004
070.4'49796'092 — dc22

                                                    2003027820

                    10 9 8 7 6 5 4 3 2 1

                            COM

        Printed in the United States of America

This book is dedicated to my Dad, whose works enrich the lives of all his readers and who led me on a journey of wonderful memories infused with love.

Acknowledgments

I want to thank more than anyone, my mother, who has provided me so much of my father's life. I also want to thank my wife, Karen, and my siblings: Marty, Pam, and Duane. I wish to thank my aunts and uncles for their input: John, Tony, Rudy, Dominic, Celeste, and my dear Aunt Mary, who recently passed away.

Also, thank you to Doug Phillips for his writings about Dad when he played for the Smiths Falls Beaver Yankees in Ontario, Canada, and Anita Martin who helped me put this story together.

Prologue

He (Bobby Canfield) glanced over his shoulder to see what Walter was doing, and almost jumped out of his skin as he saw the boy trying to light up a cigarette.

"No smoking, Walt!"

— from THE FOX STEALS HOME,
by Matt Christopher

"Hey, Matt," Jake said, "ever smoke a cigarette?"

Six-year-old Matt Christopher stared at the boy. Jake was taller than Matt and much huskier. "Me? Are you crazy? No."

Jake grinned. "I've got some dough," he said. "Come on. I'll buy a pack." Jake's parents were inside the house visiting Matt's father. That gave the boys plenty of time to head down to the local store to buy a pack of cigarettes.

"How are you going to get cigarettes?" Matt asked as the boys walked along. "You're just a kid."

"You'll see," Jake said, smiling. "I've bought them lots of times."

When they reached the store, Jake went inside. Matt stayed outside, staring up and down the street, hoping no one he knew came by. Before long, Jake came out of the store with a pack of Lucky Strikes.

Matt was astonished. "How did you do it?" he asked.

Jake gave him a smart, wise-guy grin. "I just told him it's for my father."

What a sneak! Matt thought to himself.

Matt and Jake headed back to Matt's house. Making sure the adults didn't see them, they hurried around to the backyard. Jake tore open the pack of cigarettes. He took out one and handed it to Matt, then took out another one for himself. From his pocket he took a pack of matches, lit his cigarette, and then lit Matt's.

"I can't," Matt said, holding the cigarette, shaking like a leaf in the wind. "If my father finds out —"

"How could he?" Jake cut Matt short. "I'm not gonna tell. And you're dumb if you do. Go 'head. Put it in your mouth and puff on it. Watch me."

Matt watched him take a long puff on the cigarette, hold his breath a minute, and then blow out the smoke. It was clear that Jake had done this before.

"Try it," Jake said.

Still scared but not wanting to seem like a baby, Matt put the cigarette between his lips and inhaled. At first nothing happened. Then the smoke hit his throat. Matt started to cough — and couldn't stop. As he struggled for breath, three thoughts crossed his mind. First, that his father would surely hear him hacking, discover him with a cigarette, and punish him. Second, that smoking was one of the stupidest things he'd ever tried. And third, that if he felt awful right now, it was his own fault for letting Jake talk him into doing something he knew was bad.

When his throat finally stopped burning and he could breathe again, Matt threw the cigarette on the ground and crushed it under the sole of his shoe. Then he looked at Jake through tearstained eyes and said, "Forget it. You can smoke the rest of the Luckies yourself."

3

The events of that day stuck with Matt Christopher for a long time. For one thing, he never smoked another cigarette in his life! And years later — in 1978, to be exact — that same event found its way into one of the many books for young readers that Matt Christopher authored. In fact, the situations, characters, settings, and conflicts he wrote about were often drawn from the experiences he had in his life.

Perhaps his strongest, most positive memories were of his three greatest loves: family, sports, and writing. That he was able to combine those three loves into a career that spans fifty years is a tribute to his hard work. More important, it shows his determination to pursue his dream, a dream he never lost sight of even when the odds seemed stacked against him.

Chapter One:
1917-1929

A Writer Is Born

Matthew Frederick Christopher was born on August 16, 1917, in a small mining community outside of Allentown, Pennsylvania. He was the first child of Frederick and Mary Christopher, and the first of the Christopher family to be born in the United States.

Matt's father, Frederick Cristoforo, was born in Italy on May 17, 1895. When Frederick was about ten years old, he, his father, Matteo Cristoforo, and his uncle immigrated to America. They Americanized their last name to Christopher and settled in Bath, Pennsylvania, where the men found jobs at the local cement plant.

Bath was like many other industrial communities of that era. It consisted of a downtown section with gravel streets, dirt alleys, and vacant lots, or sandlots, as they were called. The houses that surrounded the town were small bungalows with three or four rooms. Very few people could afford to buy their own home. Instead, they rented from one of the mining companies. Some houses were painted white, but most were natural wood seasoned gray over the years. The whole town was very dirty, blanketed in a thin coating of dust that traveled from the cement plant.

The same year that Frederick Christopher left Italy, ten-year-old Mary Rose Vass and her parents left their native land of Hungary to come to the United States. Like the Christophers, the Vasses were in search of the American dream. They, too, made Bath their home.

Frederick and Mary met while living in Bath. When they were old enough, they began dating. They were married in 1916 and soon after welcomed their first baby. They named him Matthew, the English version of Matteo. They called him Matt for short.

Matt was still a toddler when the Christophers made the first of many moves, from Bath to Bath Portland, another small industrial town a few miles away. Their new house was a bungalow similar to the one in Bath. It was within walking distance of the Penn-Dixie

Matt Christopher, future children's book author!

Cement Plant where both Frederick and Matteo worked.

While the men were busy putting in long days at the plant, Mary did her best to make the Christopher house a home. Some of her time was spent cleaning away the dust and dirt that constantly blew in from the plant. She also made sure to have hearty meals ready when the tired men returned home after work. The rest of her day was spent caring for the growing number of children in the Christopher family.

Matt's sister Mary was born March 3, 1919, his brother Frederick arrived April 5, 1922, and another brother, Michael, on March 17, 1924. Eventually, Frederick and Mary would have eight children. Matt, the oldest, was expected to help around the house however he could. One of his tasks was weeding the garden.

The garden was Frederick's pride and joy. It was located on the hill behind their house and was part of a four-acre plot shared by other families who rented houses from the cement company. Because supermarkets were a thing of the future, buying fresh produce was a luxury. For many families, these gardens were their primary source of vegetables. Potatoes, corn, lettuce, and green and hot peppers were the mainstays. Each fall, the vegetables were harvested, canned, and put in the cold cellar for meals in the winter.

Weeding wasn't easy, but young Matt was hardly a stranger to hard work. After all, his father and grandfather worked long hours to provide the family with the necessities of life. His mother toiled to keep the house tidy and put good food on the table. They did what they did not because they loved the work, but because they loved each member of the family and wanted them to have the best they could give. They didn't shirk their duties — and neither did Matt, not then nor as he grew older. In fact, the love of family and the strong work ethic that his father, mother, and grandfather instilled in him early on stayed with him for the rest of his life.

Much of Matt's childhood was spent moving from one small industrial town to another. In 1925, the family left Bath Portland, Pennsylvania, for Portland Point, New York, a community of fewer than twenty houses. After less than a year, they moved to Trenton, New Jersey, to a neighborhood where the buildings were so close together that neighbors could

Matt Christopher in uniform at age 12.

almost reach out a side window and touch the house next door. Two more brothers, Anthony and John, were born while the family lived in Trenton.

In 1929, when Matt was twelve, his father decided to move the family back to Bath Portland. He and Matteo got back their old jobs and found a two-story house about a mile away from where they had lived before.

Their new neighborhood was close to the quarry. Warning sirens sounded regularly, alerting people that workers were about to blast the rock. Whenever the sirens wailed, Matt and his brothers and sister knew to cover their ears — and more importantly, to get as far from the quarry as they could. Even though the blasts were carefully controlled, there was always the danger of something going wrong.

Living close to a quarry and cement plant was nothing new for Matt. But living in a house that had a reputation for being haunted was! Twenty years earlier, someone had been murdered in the house that Matt and his family now lived in. Since then, many people had reported seeing a ghost prowling in and around the dwelling.

The first time Matt saw his new home, he didn't

think it looked haunted. He thought it looked lonely. The house had been vacant and neglected for several years. The boards of the steps leading up to the porch were buckled and rickety. A single wooden chair sat next to the front entry. The screen door hung from the top hinge only. The screen itself was ripped at one corner and flapped every time the door moved.

Inside, the house was just as rundown, but after the family moved in, Mary managed to make it look and feel cheerful. Matt's parents and sister took the two downstairs bedrooms, and Matt and his brothers and grandfather took the two upstairs. Filled to the brim with Christophers, including the newest addition, Rudolph, the "lonely" house was soon transformed into a happy home. None of them really believed the rumors that the place was haunted.

Then late one night, Matt was awakened by a loud cry followed by footsteps thundering down the stairs. He and his brothers shot out of bed and rushed to the kitchen to see what was happening. His parents and sister hurried in moments later.

Matt's grandfather, his face as white as a sheet, rattled off a torrent of words in his native Italian.

Matt turned to his father and asked, "What did he say?"

"He said somebody pulled the blanket off of him," his father replied, his eyes black with fear. "And then this somebody began to shake the bed. But when he turned on the light, nobody was there."

Goose bumps formed on Matt's arms, then all over his body. He wanted the whole thing to be a bad dream — but there was his father, nodding his head and telling everyone that he, who had never feared a thing in his life, was deathly afraid of what had just happened.

Somehow, the family managed to conquer their dread and stay in the house for another year before moving to another place in town. Although there were no more hauntings, Matt never forgot his one brush with the supernatural. From that time on, he had an interest in the mysterious and unexplained.

Other than this late-night fright, Matt's life in Portland Point was pretty normal. He went to school and did his homework and chores. In his free time and during the summer vacation, he played outdoor games like hide-and-seek, kick the can, and his favorite, baseball.

Portland Point didn't have a regular ball field for kids to play on, so Matt and his friends had to make their own. The area behind Matt's house was the most open, so that's where they played. Their backstop was a woodshed built next to the Christophers' kitchen door. Flat stones were used for bases. The pitcher's mound was just a small hole in the ground. The batter's box was a square of dirt made by countless feet "digging in" before each pitch. Those same feet trampled down the lines of the base paths, especially the one between home plate and first.

Teams were usually short a few players, and since most kids wanted to play an infield position, there was always a hole in the outfield. None of the players could afford a real baseball bat, so they used a broom handle with tape around the grip to make it look like a major league bat. And since no one had a real baseball either, they used a worn tennis ball.

That tennis ball wasn't as hard as a baseball, but it still stung when it was caught barehanded. Baseball gloves were expensive, however, so any player who wanted to protect his catching hand had to make a glove from whatever materials he could scrounge.

To make his glove, Matt cut out two pieces of cardboard slightly larger than his hand. One piece was for the front of the glove, the other for the back. Next he cut two pieces of cloth to cover the cardboard. Then he took some yarn and sewed the cloth and cardboard together, leaving a hole at the bottom so he could slide his hand up into the glove. It may not have been the best glove around, but it didn't slow Matt down. He was a top-notch fielder.

Matt was also as quick as a fox around the bases. Wearing the same shoes he wore to church each Sunday, he'd clobber the ball, then sprint to first base. Once he reached first safely, he usually stole second — and many times third too! Other players learned that unless they kept an eye on Matt, he'd be in scoring position before they knew it.

These summertime games were played well into the evenings and only ended when mothers started calling their boys home. When that happened, the game quickly ended. No one wanted to get in trouble for being out too late. But before they left the field, they always vowed to meet again the next day and continue the game.

Matt never forgot the joy of playing sandlot ball. When he became a writer, he often turned to these happy memories for inspiration. But before that time, his passion for baseball and his skill at playing the game almost took him as far as a player could go — to the major leagues.

Chapter Two:
1930–1938

Major League Dreams

As the kids of the Portland Point neighborhood grew older and could wallop the ball farther, they moved the field from the Christophers' backyard to a field adjoining the neighborhood gardens. The new baseball diamond had a lot more room, but it had one drawback. It was in the local cow pasture. Not only did the players have to be on the lookout for the cows, they also had to watch where they stepped. If they weren't careful, they wound up smack in the middle of a pile of cow manure!

Matt spent as much time as he could playing baseball, honing his skills and just having fun. But it wasn't until high school that he got the chance to play for a real team. In his sophomore year, his natural ability and his unending desire to succeed at the game earned him a spot on the varsity team for Ludlowville High School.

High school baseball was a breeze for Matt. His favorite position was shortstop, covering the hole between second and third base, but he played most of the positions, including catcher. When he batted, he usually got on base — and because he was still one of the fastest runners on the field, he often stole his way to second.

Baseball was Matt's first love, but he enjoyed other sports as well. He played football for the Ludlowville team in the fall. In the winter, he played basketball, but not for the school team. Instead, he and a group of friends played pickup basketball on the second floor of an old ramshackle barn.

Like the field where he used to play sandlot baseball, the barn basketball court was far from perfect. The barn was owned by the cement company and had to be cleared of all the junk the company had left there before the boys could even think about playing. The floor sagged in the middle and creaked whenever anyone ran on it. The baskets were the rims of hay-wagon wheels, nailed to the walls. The only spectators they had were the rodents that ran across the court during games. Still, the barn was dry and gave them a place to play during the winter. Until springtime and baseball season, that was better than nothing.

As much as he loved sports, Matt couldn't afford to spend all his free time playing them. His father had steady work at the cement plant, and with the birth of Matt's sister Celeste in early 1932, there were eleven Christophers to feed. Making ends meet was often difficult.

Matt, the eldest child, knew it was time to start helping out. When he was fourteen years old, he began to make some money by selling magazine subscriptions. Most of his earnings went to his parents, but he did keep a little for himself.

Going door to door asking people to buy subscriptions was not an easy task. But there were a few pluses to his job. For one thing, he was practically his own boss. And for another, he got to read all the magazines he sold.

Matt loved to read just as much as he loved to play sports. He pored over each magazine from cover to cover, devouring tales of adventure, mystery, and horror. He read detective stories and stories about sports. As he turned the pages, he dreamed of visiting the places he read about and having exciting adventures.

But his dream didn't end there. As he read story after story, Matt began to realize how powerful the written word was. With just a few sentences in an adventure story, he could be transported to another world, another time. Ghost stories could make his spine tingle, even though he was safe in his own room. He could test his wits and solve a crime alongside the detective he was reading about.

To be able to write good stories, he thought, must be a wonderful talent to have. And not just write them, but to get paid for writing them, too! And before he was even out of high school, Matt Christopher began to wonder if maybe writing stories was something he could do. To be a writer — that became his ultimate dream.

Matt knew it wasn't going to be easy to make his dream a reality. In fact, there was already an obstacle in his path. He didn't have a typewriter. Matt was certain that all real writers had typewriters. Not having one was going to hold him back.

But typewriters were expensive, and the Christopher family was far from rich. Somehow, Matt convinced his father that he wouldn't be able to sell stories unless they were typewritten. They drove to Ithaca, New York, together and purchased an eighteen-dollar Barr-Morse typewriter.

Eighteen dollars was a lot of money for Frederick Christopher to spend. He parted with the money reluctantly, half-certain that it was going to waste — not because he didn't believe his son's desire to write, but because he believed his son's future lay somewhere other than writing.

Frederick had watched his oldest boy play baseball for years. He'd seen how Matt's fielding and batting skills had improved until he was one of the best players on any team he joined. He knew how fast his son could run. And he knew how much Matt loved sports. When he added all these things together, Frederick came to one conclusion: Matt Christopher had a future playing professional baseball.

Frederick had another reason for hoping his son would make a career out of baseball. In 1934, the United States was in the grip of the Great Depression,

Matt Christopher, 18, far right, with one of his
many championship baseball teams.

an economic nightmare that had begun in 1929. Money and jobs were scarce. People everywhere were going hungry. A cloud of despair hung over the nation.

In the midst of the bleak situation, one ray of light shone brightly: baseball. The 1920s had produced some of the greatest baseball players ever. Babe Ruth, Rogers Hornsby, Lou Gehrig, and other future Hall-of-Famers were hailed as heroes by the public. When Americans watched their heroes play, they escaped the hardships they faced every day.

Frederick believed that his oldest son would one day earn a place among these baseball giants. He had a dream that Matt would help his country through the dark time of the Depression. He also knew that if Matt succeeded in baseball, he could help his own family financially. For in 1934, like so many other families, the Christophers were having great difficulty making ends meet.

During the Depression, factories and mills around the country had to shut their doors, leaving their workers without jobs. The cement plant where Frederick and Matteo Christopher worked was no exception.

In the summer of 1934, Frederick needed to find work to support his family. Luckily, he, Matteo, and Matt all found jobs as part of a road construction crew. They earned the same amount of money, twelve and half dollars per week, all of which went toward keeping the family clothed, sheltered, and fed.

Seventeen-year-old Matt was hired as a water boy. His job was to keep the water bucket filled and to carry it to the workers so that they could drink from the bucket's ladle. The summer sun was often brutally hot, and the road construction was dry, dusty work. Matt earned every penny of his weekly wage running from worker to worker with a full bucket of water.

As exhausting as the job was, Matt suffered from more than the heat. Many of the workers he brought water to insulted him regularly, calling him a "Wop," an ethnic slur for people of Italian heritage. Matt burned each time someone called him that, but he did his job without complaint because he knew his meager wages were vital to his family. Still, he made a vow never to use such words himself. He knew how badly they could hurt.

Matt was always tired at the end of a workday, yet he managed to find energy to pursue other interests.

Matt wearing the Cayuga Rock Salt uniform.

He learned to play the banjo and spent many nights on the back porch of the Christopher house plucking out chords and singing songs. And throughout the summer, he played baseball.

The road-construction job lasted all the summer and into the first two months of Matt's senior year in high school. In that same year, he took the first step toward fulfilling Frederick's dream. He signed a contract to play with the Cayuga Rock Salts, a semi-professional baseball team sponsored by the Cayuga Rock Salt company. He played his favorite position, shortstop, with them throughout his senior year. Since he also continued to play for the Ludlowville High School team, he had plenty of opportunities to sharpen his skills.

In 1935 Matt graduated from high school. He had high hopes of getting into Cornell University, but it was not to be. Although his grades had been good, he lacked a required mathematics credit needed to get into college. To get the credit, he would have to go to night school, and that was not something his father could afford. Besides, in Frederick's opinion, college was too expensive. Matt was from a poor family; a job was what he needed.

Finding work wasn't difficult. As a member of the Rock Salt team, Matt was offered a job at the Cayuga Rock Salt mine. Because he was under twenty-one, he was given a job near the top floor in the breaking building rather than in the mine itself. All he had to do was sit in front of a conveyor belt and pick out impurities from the salt as it passed by him. For this, Matt earned sixteen dollars a week. He kept one dollar and gave the rest to his parents.

Before long, Matt's days were divided between working for the Cayuga Rock Salt mine and playing shortstop for the Cayuga Rock Salt team. Thanks in large part to his lightning-quick speed, catlike reflexes, and strong batting, the Cayuga Rock Salts achieved a reputation for being one of the best semi-professional baseball teams in the state.

Frederick watched his son play with great satisfaction. He was one of Matt's most supportive fans — but also one of his chief critics. When Matt played well, his father patted him on the back, smiled, and said, "My boy, you're the best." But when Matt played a poor game, Frederick just looked at him and said, "Son, you were lousy. If I was the manager, I would have kept you on the bench."

Life might have continued in this same vein, but in the spring of 1936, Matt had a surprising visit from a friend of the family. The man was a former semi-pro baseball player and manager of a team in the Ithaca City league. He told Matt that Johnny Haddock, manager of a professional baseball team in the Canadian-American League called the Smiths Falls Beavers — Class C, to be exact — had seen Matt play. Haddock had been impressed and wanted to sign Matt to his team.

Matt was shocked. The Beavers were a farm team for the New York Yankees! Could it be that Frederick was right, that Matt was destined for the major leagues after all?

The next day, Johnny Haddock offered Matt a contract worth seventy-five dollars a month, plus expenses paid on the road. Matt knew the offer was decent, but bet he could do better. He held out for eighty-five dollars — and got it. A few days later, he hugged his parents and siblings good-bye and boarded a bus bound for Smiths Falls, Ontario. It was the first week of May 1936, and Matt Christopher was officially a professional baseball player.

The first people Matt met when he arrived in

Smiths Falls were his roommate, a pitcher from Syracuse, New York, and four other young men who lived in the same multi-room boarding house. Most of the players were from upstate New York. In fact, two of his teammates were players whom he had competed against in the past, so they were not all strangers. That made being away from home a little bit easier.

One of those players gave Matt an odd piece of advice. "Put your age down as seventeen, not nineteen," the player said. "Major league teams look for young guys." Figuring such a little lie wouldn't hurt anyone, Matt did as his teammate suggested.

The first two weeks in Smiths Falls were a blur. The manager was a hard-nosed man who took his job very seriously. His players were there to play baseball, and that was it.

Matt soon found out just how strict that rule was. One evening he was reading a magazine in the lobby of the hotel in which they were staying. All of a sudden, the magazine was snatched out of his hands. Startled, he looked up to see his manager glaring at him.

"Christopher," the manager snapped, "you're here

to play baseball, eat baseball, and talk baseball. Not to read. Understand?"

Matt was so tongue-tied, all he could do was nod. From then on, he tried to put everything but baseball out of his head. And at first, it seemed that his focus and determination were paying off. In his first exhibition game, the local newspaper reported that "starring honors were stolen neatly and completely by Matty Christopher, the dark seventeen-year-old kid who held down third base. Christy whacked in two runs with a wow of a triple, beat out a dribbler for another hit, and contributed a flashy, barehanded stop to rob Joe Mooney of a single."

Unfortunately, Matt was unable to follow up this outstanding performance in the weeks that followed. While he played well enough in the field, hitting against major league–bound pitchers proved difficult. A few months after joining the Beavers, he was released from his contract. He returned home, feeling defeated.

But professional baseball wasn't quite ready to give up on Matt just yet. Soon after his return, he received a call from the manager of Brockport, a team that was in the same league as Smiths Falls. The Brockport manager had seen Matt play and thought he showed potential. He offered Matt a spot on his team.

Matt gave the offer serious thought. He knew he was being given a second chance to make it in the big leagues. But by then, he wasn't sure he had what it took to succeed in professional ball. He turned the offer down, reasoning that if he wasn't good enough for Smiths Falls, he wasn't good enough for Brockport.

It was a very tough decision for Matt and one that he regretted making more than once. But baseball wasn't out of his life entirely. A few months after turning Brockport down, he was approached by the manager of the Moose baseball team to play for them in the Ithaca City league. No money was offered, but because Matt still wanted to play baseball, he agreed to join.

Matt played with the Moose team for a year. His performance was strong enough that it caught the eye of Charlie Foote, the manager of Freeville-Dryden, another team in the Ithaca City League. Foote offered him money to manage and play for his team. Matt accepted.

Despite some rocky moments — Matt injured his left knee twice while sliding into second on a steal — the season with Freeville-Dryden was the best of Matt's career. Fans loved watching him sprint around the bases and applauded each time the switch hitter sent the ball flying over the infielders' heads.

Matt found out just how much the fans appreciated his heads-up play at the end of the season. Before one of the last games, Charlie Foote called him out of the dugout. With his arm around his star player's shoulders, Charlie asked Matt to accept a special jacket as an award for being selected the most valuable player of the year by the fans of Freeville-Dryden.

As moving as that moment was, it was overshadowed by something that happened soon after. Matt was tapped to play in an exhibition baseball game against the New York Giants, one of the best teams in the National Baseball League. Matt could hardly believe it when he got the news. He would be facing such formidable players as Bob Seeds, Dick Bartell, Mel Ott, Johnny Wittig, and Bill Terry!

The game, a fund-raiser for a memorial to former Giants manager John J. McGraw, was played on

Most Valuable Player for the
Freeville-Dryden team in 1938.

Monday, August 8, 1938, in Truxton, New York. Matt managed to get a hit off pitcher Johnny Wittig his first time up, and then grounded out while batting against Bill Terry. He only played five innings, and their team lost 8–1, but that all was immaterial. To play against future Hall-of-Famers before a crowd of 10,000 people was the greatest thrill of Matt's baseball career. And as it turned out, it was the closest he would get to playing in the major leagues.

Chapter Three:
1939–1951

Small Steps Forward

Baseball was a constant for Matt Christopher in the late 1930s. But it was not the only thing in his life.

Pursuing a writing career continued to be his greatest goal. And every so often, he would get a small taste of what such a career might be like. Back in 1935, the Christopher family had been living in a small, two-story house in a charming neighborhood in Ithaca. Matt loved the neighborhood so much that he used it as the setting for a short story idea he was developing. He submitted his finished work to a *Writer's Digest* short-short story contest — and to his amazement and delight, it was selected as one of two hundred winners. The story never sold, but Matt hoped that it marked the beginning of his career.

Not long after this milestone, the Christopher family moved out of Ithaca to the nearby town of

CERTIFICATE of MERIT

awarded annually

by WRITER'S DIGEST

for distinctive ability in creative writing

TO _Matthew F. Christopher_

RICHARD K. ABBOTT
Editor-in-Chief

ARON M. MATHIEU
Business Manager

Member the United Press

WRITER'S DIGEST
Leading, Largest and Foremost Writer's Magazine

22 EAST TWELFTH STREET   CINCINNATI

April 22, 1938

Dear Mr. Christopher:

Here, at long last, is the Certificate of Merit, you won in the last WRITER'S DIGEST contest. We are happy and proud to include you as one of the 200 winners. Your winning script is going with me to New York this month and I will work to place it for you. (Should this be against your wishes please write me.) I am leaving tardily due to press of business at our own office.

A fault with most of the scripts in the contest, winners as well as losers, is that the writer fails to give the reader any credit for intelligence and smears each new fact into the reader's brain with a big obvious smudge. That plus the confusing of an "incident" with a genuine plot were the major things that caused many of the scripts to miss.

To place as high as you did in our contest is no mean feat as contestants included hundreds of well known writers. A victory such as this is important, and I know it will serve to re-affirm your confidence in yourself. I urge you to study the masters of good writing so as to improve your own work. I hope to see a good deal more of it, and in print, too.

Sincerely,

A. M. Mathieu

Also publishers of: Radio Dial, Independent Salesman, Automobile Digest, American Building Association News, Sportsmen's Horizon, Gasoline Dealer, Radio Log Book and Writer's Year Book.

Matt's very first acceptance letter — and his
Certificate of Merit from *Writer's Digest.*

Lansing. Less than a week later, Matt happened to see a young boy and a teenage girl trying to fly a model glider. Like a kite, the glider was on a string held by the boy. The girl ran and when the string tautened, she released the glider into the air. Once the glider was airborne, the boy coaxed it into making wide, sweeping arcs around the field. Then he guided it down to a perfect three-point landing.

Matt was impressed by the flight, but he was even more impressed with the girl. She was one of the most beautiful girls he had ever seen.

Her name was Catherine Krupa, and soon after they met they began dating. Since Cay, as Matt called her, was still in school and Matt was busy working and playing ball, they only saw each other on Friday or Saturday nights. This went on for a few years, until one day, Matt's mother said to him, "You better marry that girl. She likes you."

Matt had already made up his mind that Cay was the girl he wanted to spend his life with. Cay felt the same way about him. He proposed, she accepted, and they were married on July 13, 1940.

The newlyweds bought a house right next door to her parents. It had two bedrooms upstairs, a

The wedding of Catherine Krupa (in white, fifth from left) to Matt Christopher (center) on July 13, 1940.

bathroom, and a kitchen with a dining area and a living room downstairs. There was a one-car garage and sufficient land to plant a garden and build a chicken house. During the weekdays, Cay kept house and Matt worked in the factory of the Allen-Wales Adding Machine Manufacturing Company in Ithaca. After work, Matt played baseball and softball. And after that, he worked on his writing.

Not all of his writing time was spent making up stories. Often, Matt simply read stories for enjoyment. Then he analyzed them, too, word by word, sentence by sentence, paragraph by paragraph. He cut out the beginnings and endings of stories in magazines, pasted them in a scrapbook, and studied them over and over.

Hoping that it would help make his dream a reality, Matt took a primary course in writing and subscribed to writing magazines. He quickly realized that writing was not any ordinary job. For one thing, there was no specific requirement in order to write. Even with a college degree, there was no guarantee that a person would be able to write a story and then sell it. Degrees didn't create the mind and the soul of a writer.

Yet another championship team. Matt is fourth from the right in the second row.

Matt also knew that there were thousands of other writers who were trying to get published. He knew from reading writer's magazines that rejection was the norm for most hopeful authors. Many who were rejected became so discouraged they quit trying. Matt realized that if he was going to succeed, he had to grow a thick skin.

But above all, Matt understood that he had to set aside time each day to work at his craft. So even after long days at the factory and evenings on the ball field, he spent most nights at his typewriter. He wrote dozens of stories ranging from romances to horror tales and one-act plays.

Cay knew from the very beginning that her husband wanted to be a writer. She never questioned his dream and supported everything that he wanted to do to achieve that goal. She left him alone when he was writing, even though it often meant not seeing him for hours at a time. Like Matt, she hoped that in time he would be able to support them by writing.

One day in the summer of 1941, Matt saw an advertisement in a writer's magazine. Greenburg Publishers of New York was seeking submissions for a book of one hundred one-act plays. Writers would

41

be paid a flat fee if their plays were accepted. Matt decided to submit *Escape,* the best of three plays he had written. To his great delight, Greenburg accepted *Escape,* and soon after sent Matt a contact. He would be paid five dollars or he could accept payment in the form of the book when it was published. Five dollars was a nice fee, but for the sale of his first published work, Matt chose the book instead.

When Matt received the book with his play in it, he called for Cay to join him. Together, they flipped to the table of contents. There it was: "*Escape,* by Matthew F. Christopher." He and Cay were thrilled to see his name in print. They both hoped that that play was the start of a long line of published works.

About a year after this first sale, Cay and Matt welcomed their first baby. Martin Allen was born on September 15, 1942. Marty, as he was called, was a great joy to both parents. Cay devoted much of her time to caring for him while making sure that Matt still had the freedom he needed to focus on his writing.

And write he did! Detective stories had long been a favorite of his, and in the early forties there were scores of magazines that published such tales. Matt

Matt, Cay, and baby Martin.

Reading was a top priority in the Christopher
household. Here, Cay reads to Marty.

As busy as Matt was writing and working,
he always made time for family. Here he is
with Marty in 1945.

was determined to write and sell at least one detective story. So throughout the winter of 1942 and the spring of 1943, he wrote and submitted a detective story a week for forty weeks.

At first, the mail brought nothing but rejection slips. Then one day in the summer of 1943, Matt received a letter from a magazine publishing company called Fiction House, Inc.:

Dear Mr. Christopher,

I like your story, "Clue of the Missing Finger," and shall be very glad to use it in the next issue of Detective Story Magazine. *As you are a new writer with us I would appreciate a reference or two from some other editor. Upon receipt of same I will shoot you a check for fifty dollars.*

> *Cordially yours,*
> *Malcolm Reiss*
> *Editor*

Matt was thrilled. He immediately sat down and wrote to Mr. Reiss. He provided a list of editors whom he had received letters from, even though they were rejections. Within weeks, a check for fifty

Matt with the check for fifty dollars from "The Missing Finger Points" — his very first sale!

dollars arrived in the mail. He could hardly wait to see his story in print.

Fiction House did not send Matt a copy of the story, however. So month after month he went to the local newsstand and pored over the latest edition of *Detective Story Magazine* to see if his story was there. Finally, he saw it. The publisher had changed the title to "The Missing Finger Points," but that didn't matter to Matt. What mattered was that he had once again been published. The question now was, could he do it again?

He had his answer before the year's end. *Our Navy,* a magazine dedicated to people interested in naval warfare, accepted his story "The Target Downstairs." The magazine paid a penny a word for the 3,000-word story, or $30, not a lot of money. But having the story accepted taught Matt just how important it was to get the details right. Before writing the story, he had researched submarines, aircraft carriers, and other naval vessels. His story included many accurate details; it was those details as much as the story line itself that had caught the editor's eyes. In fact, the details were so right-on that the editor thought Matt was an ex-Navy officer.

Matt and Cay continued to be optimistic about Matt's writing career. But unfortunately, 1944 was not a banner year. Although Matt managed to sell three more short stories to *Our Navy,* he received rejection after rejection from other publishers. The following year wasn't any better. Only three more short stories sold of the many that he sent out. His dream of a career writing books seemed to be fading away.

Other factors added to the gloomy time. The world was in the throes of World War II, and some of Matt's brothers were on their way overseas to fight. Matt, on the other hand, worked on bombsights at the factory. Since the manufacture of these specialized items aided the war effort, he was given a deferment and didn't have to go into active service.

Matt struggled with the fact that he was not in combat overseas. He knew that thousands of young men, including his own brothers, were fighting to preserve the right for people to fulfill their dreams. His sense of honor and love for his country were strong. His parents had made their way to America to fulfill their dream, and Matt knew how important that was to them and now to him.

Before the war was over, Matt declined his fourth

deferment and enlisted in the Army. Now he faced a different struggle: the pain of going to war and leaving his family behind. Days before he was to depart, his friends and family gave him a send-off party. Then, just before he was scheduled to leave, a postcard arrived telling him that his departure had been delayed one month.

Before that month was over, peace was declared. Since the war had ended, Matt was notified that he did not have to report to duty. Mixed emotions settled in again. He was relieved that he did not have to go through boot camp or to a ship overseas, yet he still felt guilty, as if somehow he had shirked his duty to serve his country.

After the war, it didn't take long for life in the Christopher household to return to its previous routine. Matt changed jobs twice, first taking a position in the assembly department of the Smith-Corona typewriter plant in Groton, New York, then returning to Allen-Wales, now owned by the National Cash Register Company. He also spent more time at his desk, writing, sending out stories — and receiving more rejections than acceptances.

That pattern was the norm over the next few years.

From left to right: Marty, Cay, Dale, Pamela, and Matt.

Matt sold ten stories for every fifty he sent out, not a bad percentage of acceptances, but at an average of fifteen dollars a story, he was far from making a living at writing. The brightest times occurred when the Christopher family got bigger. Pamela Jean was born on Valentine's Day 1946, and the following May, Dale Robin was born.

Matt and Cay's house was now too small for their family of five to live in. So in 1947, Matt borrowed money to build a bigger home on a half-acre lot adjacent to their current home. Although both Cay and Matt enjoyed having the extra space — Matt had his own study for the first time — paying for the new house became a burden. The money from Matt's job wasn't enough to pay the mortgage and all the bills they had. As their debts mounted each month, their financial situation started to cause a very big strain in their lives. More than ever, they looked to the publication of Matt's stories for extra income.

By this time, Matt had sold more than fifty short stories, but still nothing was happening that led him to believe that he could make a living just on these short-story sales. In fact, it was just the opposite. All of the rejection letters pointed to an unending pattern of failure. Matt couldn't help but doubt his ability.

Then one day a letter came that changed that pattern. It was from Delores Lehr, editor of *Farm and Ranch* magazine:

I wish I could buy all three of the stories you recently submitted. I especially liked "Chuck in Our Backyard." But unfortunately, we are looking for one particular kind of story now.

Due to the fact that we publish only one story a month, we must have a variety in our short stories, so we are on the look-out for a "young love" or a story about a little boy . . . for our Christmas issue. Perhaps you have something that would fit. You have a talent for writing about children . . . and children are the most difficult subjects to capture with a pen. I firmly believe that you will be selling regularly very soon. Your writing is smooth, terse, and appealing.

Delores Lehr, Editor of Farm and Ranch

This was a rejection letter unlike any Matt had received before. He had never considered writing for or about children before. But now, Delores Lehr's words sparked him to try. He started writing and submitting short stories to such magazines as *Teen Time, Young People, Famous Funnies, Treasure Chest, Fun and Facts for Children,* and *Story Trails.* The short stories were longer, as many as 4,000 words — and they were selling. Soon, profits from these stories were helping to pay the mortgage. More important, they helped Matt through a rough time during which he believed he'd never become a professional writer.

In the end, however, these earnings did not come close to the amount of money he received working at National Cash Register. He realized that if he was ever going to quit his job and write full time, he would have to write something that would pay much better than a penny a word.

Mysteries had always interested him, so he set out to write a mystery novel. To get a feel for the genre, he read every mystery novel he could get his hands on. Once he came up with an idea on his own, he spent as much time as possible working out the details. During his lunch hour from the factory, he sat in his car and plotted out the story while he ate. He then worked into all hours of the night, writing and typing up his tale.

A full year and some sixty-thousand words later, Matt finished his first full-length novel. It was called *Lay the Body Anywhere.* He knew that getting a novel published was much different than getting a short story accepted by a magazine. Getting a book editor merely to read his work would be challenging. So he contacted an agent to help him get his foot in the doors of publishing companies.

The agent read the manuscript and wrote back that the book was good, but that it needed some revision if it was to sell. He'd help Matt with the revision, but it would cost a fee of fifty dollars.

Matt was desperate to sell the novel, so he agreed. He sent the agent a check and received the manuscript back with a long list of suggestions. Matt reworked the story, sent it back, and waited.

Months went by with no word from the agent. All of Matt's hard work — plus fifty dollars of his money — seemed to be for nothing. At the end of their rope financially, Matt and Cay were forced to sell their new house. Then they packed everyone up and moved to Syracuse, New York, where they hoped they'd have a better chance at making a living.

The move was hard for Matt, Cay, and the children. Syracuse was a big city filled with strangers. They all missed living close to their families. And on top of it all, Matt felt like a failure for letting his own family down. Both he and Cay prayed that things would turn around for them soon.

Matt and Cay purchased a large, two-story building in the north side of Syracuse. Downstairs were two storefronts with a two-bedroom apartment at the rear of the building. There was another apartment upstairs. The plan was to live in the downstairs apartment and rent the upstairs one. They could also collect rent from the plumbing and heating company run out of one of the storefronts. Cay intended to turn the other store into a gift shop.

The neighborhood was much different from the one they had lived in before. Although there was a park nearby where Matt and his sons could play a game of catch, their street was very crowded. Their building was sandwiched between a meat market and a dry cleaner. The backyard was enclosed by a

Matt is ready to play a game of catch in the
park near their house in Syracuse.

Matt poses with his new car.

high iron fence and big bushes. On the other side of the fence were tenant apartments. The yards of these apartments were piled high with junk, as if people just threw things back there with no intention of ever picking any of it up.

Matt was hopeful that the sales of his stories plus the rental income and profits from the gift shop would be enough for the family to live on. So instead of finding a full-time job, he spent the next two years writing short stories for magazines.

Unfortunately, the plan didn't work out. The gift shop struggled to make money, and in 1951 Matt sold only two short stories. The next year, he sold thirteen, but that was not enough. Matt had to find work if the family was to survive.

After days of searching the classifieds in the newspapers, he finally found a job selling umbrellas and other household products door to door. The job was degrading for a man who was bright and envisioned himself as a writer. After two weeks he quit and landed another job driving a laundry truck for a dry-cleaning firm. He earned fifty dollars a week plus twelve-and-a-half percent commission for every new account he added. The job brought in more than a hundred dollars per week, but the hours were long and left little time or energy for the creative process of writing. Matt's dream of becoming a writer seemed less certain than ever.

Then one day he struck up a conversation with one of his customers, a foreman at the General Electric plant. Matt expressed an interest in getting work at the plant. In a matter of days, he had filled out the application and had been offered a job on the assembly line, installing the backs onto televisions. Matt accepted the offer and gave his notice at the dry-cleaning firm. A week later he was working for GE.

The job was extremely easy — and boring. To help pass the time, Matt started thinking up humorous verses, short four-, six-, and eight-liners that played with the sounds and meanings of words. He had fun writing them and submitted them to various magazines, but none of them sold.

Matt didn't stay on the assembly line for long. He told his foreman about his experience building adding machines and typewriters. Within two months, he had been promoted. The Christopher fortunes were finally turning around.

Look for the Body, published in 1952.

And the promotion was not the only good news. A few months later, Matt received a letter from his agent telling him that his mystery novel, *Lay the Body Anywhere*, had been sold to the Phoenix Press.

Matt could scarcely believe it. He had sold his first novel!

He received an advance of one hundred and fifty dollars. If the book, now titled *Look for the Body*, sold more than 2,500 copies, he would receive ten percent of all sales. Sadly, that never happened. The hundred and fifty dollars was all the money that book would ever make.

Still, Matt was encouraged by the sale. He took it as proof that he could write well enough to be published in book form. Perhaps, he thought, he just needed to find his niche, to discover what kind of book he was best at writing. But if it wasn't mysteries, what was it?

Chapter Four:
1952-1963

A Career Is Born

One day in the fall of 1952, Matt was talking with a local librarian. In the course of the conversation, she mentioned how unfortunate it was that there were so few sports books for young readers. Boys in particular lacked good books, she said, and she believed sports novels that featured children might peak their interest.

Suddenly, Matt recalled the letter he had received from Delores Lehr. "You have a talent for writing about children . . ." she'd written. And if there was one thing Matt Christopher knew inside and out, it was sports. He was inspired.

Over Thanksgiving weekend, while Cay took the three children back to Lansing to visit relatives, Matt wrote a sixty-page baseball book. Titled *The Lucky*

Bat, the story was about a young boy named Marvin who wanted to get on a team — any team — and play baseball. After striking out over and over, Marvin started using a bat that seemed capable of helping him do what no other bat could: get hits.

When the book was done, Matt dug out an article he'd saved that mentioned the names of a few noted publishers who were looking for sports books for young readers. He carefully packaged up his manuscript to send out — but then he hesitated. Although he was satisfied with the story, he wasn't sure any of the publishers would take the time to read his work. Then he realized he'd never know unless he tried. He decided to send his manuscript to Little, Brown and Company, the publisher of one of his favorite books, *Good-bye, Mr. Chips,* by James Hilton.

Weeks went by without a word. Then, soon after the start of 1953, he received a reply from Helen L. Jones, the head of Little, Brown's children's book department. As he read the letter, his heart started thumping.

July 22, 1952

Dear Mr. Christopher:

I am pleased to tell you that we are very interested in the possibilities of your little story, THE LUCKY BAT. We feel, however, that before we could be in a position actually to offer you a contract we ought to be assured that you would be willing to make or to let us make certain revisions which seem necessary if we are to offer it successfully to our market.

For example, to bring out the true flavor of the persons and locality of your story you have used the typical grammar faults of your Little League characters. I would hope to find a way to achieve the same atmosphere without the grammar faults. I would also hope to make this a story for the very youngest baseball ages, say 7 to 9-year-olds, by simplifying the vocabulary wherever possible.

One of our readers is anxious about the accuracy of the Little League aspect of the story. He feels the practice sessions should be somewhat better organized and not just scrub play in which a group of kids stand together fighting to see who catches the ball. This reader also suggests, and I agree with him on both counts, that if Marvin is actually a poor boy whose family cannot buy him a glove or bat that family should not have a television set. I realize that they probably would have in this day and age, but that fact is somehow inexplicable to child readers and therefore better omitted.

We also think the title should be changed to THE LUCKY BASEBALL BAT to avoid any uncertainty as to the kind of bat.

These points are minor and easily adjusted to be sure, but I want to raise them now because unfortunately I do not know you or your aims and particular hopes for this story, and it seems most desirable to become acquainted with both you and them before we go further.

Sincerely yours,

Helen L. Jones

Helen L. Jones

HLJ/bh

Mr. Matt Christopher
302 Park Street
Syracuse 8, New York

The first of many letters from Little, Brown and Company.

Matt was grinning from ear to ear by the time he finished the letter. He quickly dashed off a reply telling Helen Jones that he was more than willing to make the necessary revisions and adjustments. He agreed with the change in title, too. Then he poured out his true feelings: that he hoped this story would launch him into a career of writing books for children. He mailed the letter, then tried to put it out of his mind.

The next letter he received from Little, Brown offered him a contract. If he agreed to the terms, he would receive an advance of $250. That sum was more than he had ever received for a single piece of work — and certainly more than he had ever gotten for only a few days' work! More important, it was possible that he had finally found his perfect genre. If all went well with *The Lucky Baseball Bat*, perhaps Matt Christopher could continue writing sports books for young readers.

The Lucky Baseball Bat was published in 1954. That same year, Helen Jones sent Matt a card, telling him that she was going to a book convention out west and would like to stop in Syracuse to discuss other book plans.

302 Park St.
Syracuse 8, N. Y.
July 24, 1952

Little, Brown & Company
c/o Miss Helen L. Jones
34 Beacon St.
Boston 6, Mass.

Dear Miss Jones:

I was thrilled to receive your letter expressing
your interest in my story, THE LUCKY BAT!

Since you raised the question, my aims and particular
hopes for this story is to launch me into a career
of writing books for children and at the same time
enjoy the vicarious thrill that goes into the writing
of them.   Please feel free to make whatever revisions
you believe are necessary on the manuscript.   The
points you mentioned are important, and from what
I see now making those adjustments will certainly
improve the story.

I realize the point in suggesting the title to
be changed to THE LUCKY BASEBALL BAT, too, and it's
okay.

If you would like to know something about my writing
background I'll be glad to give it to you.   I have
had about fifty stories published, mostly juveniles.
A few of the magazines that have accepted stories
are the following: THE CATHOLIC BOY, TREASURE CHEST,
FAMOUS FUNNIES, STORY TRAILS, YOUNG PEOPLE, MANNA,
Some of the adult magazines are DETECTIVE BOOK,
OUR NAVY, JUDY'S, SUNSHINE MAGAZINE.

An adult mystery novel was published in February.

If there are any questions, please feel free to
write me.

Cordially

Matt Christopher

Matt Christopher

Matt's heartfelt reply to Helen L. Jones.

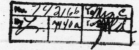

WESTERN UNION

W. P. MARSHALL, PRESIDENT

The filing time shown in the date line on telegrams and day letters is STANDARD TIME at point of origin. Time of receipt is STANDARD TIME at point of destination

SYA244 BA207

B-LLD068 PD=WUX BOSTON MASS 25 1953 MAY 25 AM 11 22   L L A

=MATT CHRISTOPHER=

=302 PARK ST SYRACUSE 8 NY=

=PLEASE SEND FIRST VERSION LUCKY BASEBALL BAT FOR
COMPARISON WITH REVISION=

    HELEN L JONES LITTLE BROWN AND CO=

THE COMPANY WILL APPRECIATE SUGGESTIONS FROM ITS PATRONS CONCERNING ITS SERVICE

Telegram from Little, Brown.

THE LUCKY BASEBALL BAT

MATT CHRISTOPHER

ILLUSTRATED BY ROBERT HENNEBERGER

The original cover of Matt's first book with Little, Brown.

Matt was thrilled. After one book, he was about to meet his editor face to face. He had once read that such encounters did not happen that often, even for well-published authors.

But as the day of the meeting drew closer, Matt's emotions changed from excited to nervous. What if things didn't go well? Maybe Helen Jones, the children's book editor of one of the top publishing houses in the country, wouldn't like him or his ideas.

Matt's nervousness lasted up to the point that he and Helen actually met. Conversation flowed smoothly and easily over lunch at the Syracuse Hotel. Matt outlined some new story ideas. Helen reacted with enthusiasm. She said she thought that they had good publishing possibilities and asked him to write up the first and mail it to her. She also advised him to take his time in putting the story together.

Matt realized that was her way of warning him that just because Little, Brown had published him once, there was no guarantee they'd take his next story. He'd have to work hard to earn another contract. Undaunted, he left the lunch ready to do just that.

His evenings and weekends were once again

consumed with writing. He and Cay had long since moved the family from the small first-floor apartment to the larger one on the second floor, so he had space for his typewriter and writing materials. He spent as much time as possible in that space, working on his newest novel.

No Baseball Allowed was the title of his second manuscript. It featured a conflict between two boys who never got along from the moment they met. He included many details from his own childhood, including descriptions of sandlot baseball games.

Matt thought that he had another winner, but he soon found out he was wrong. Helen Jones returned the manuscript. "The story seems to miss the immediate appeal of *The Lucky Baseball Bat*," she wrote, "and we are quite sure we should not be able to do well with it. . . . You are at perfect liberty to submit it elsewhere."

Another rejection. At first, Matt was depressed. Then he remembered how interested Helen had seemed in his story ideas during their lunch. He shrugged off his sense of failure and set to work on a new idea.

In the meantime, after five years in Syracuse,

Matt and Cay had had enough of living in the big city. They sold the building and headed back to Lansing, where they built a three-bedroom, single-story home on three acres of land.

Having worked for General Electric in Syracuse, Matt had no trouble securing a job as a technical editor at the GE laboratory in Ithaca. He was happy for the steady income and even happier when Cay gave birth to their fourth child, Duane Francis, in August of 1955. Yet now that he had another mouth to feed, he couldn't help but wonder if he would ever be able to quit his nine-to-five job and succeed as a full-time writer.

Soon after the Christopher clan was settled into their new home, Matt completed another book, *Baseball Pals,* and submitted it to Little, Brown. The story featured a conflict Matt thought many young readers would identify with.

In the story, Jimmie, captain of the Planets, makes himself the team's pitcher and tells his best friend, Paul, who is a good pitcher, to play center field. He is surprised and angry when Paul decides to become the pitcher for an opposing team, the Rockets. Jimmie soon realizes that even after countless practice sessions, he doesn't have the same skill on the mound as Paul. The Planets need Paul back if they are to be a winning team, but first Jimmie must swallow his pride.

Matt had worked hard to "see" the story through his characters' eyes, to make the characters' emotions seem true to life. He also included exciting play-by-play baseball action. To make sure this action was accurate, he plotted out each inning, noting when and how outs were made, who was on base when, and what kind of hits, errors, and special plays advanced the game. He believed that this book would be on target and hoped that Helen Jones would accept it.

She did. *Baseball Pals* was published in 1956. But even before the book's release, Matt was hard at work on another sports story. Once again, he looked to details in his own life to give his tale an authentic ring.

Growing up, both Matt and Cay had attended church every Sunday. Now, as parents, they made sure their whole family went to church, too. Marty, their oldest son, had a good singing voice, and so he joined the church choir.

Marty was also a good basketball player. He played

for the school team. Sometimes, basketball games and practices conflicted with choir rehearsals, and he had to choose which one to attend.

When Matt decided to write a basketball story, he created a main character, Kim, who, like Marty, had to choose between playing basketball and singing in the choir. He called the manuscript *Mr. Biddy Basketball,* named for a real basketball organization.

Shortly after mailing the manuscript to Little, Brown, Matt realized that the Biddy League Basketball just might not like the idea of him using their name in his book without their permission. He wrote to the Biddy League authorities, and soon received a curt reply telling him that he could not use their name in his book.

Matt contacted Helen Jones immediately and told her of this unfortunate development. He felt terrible for not checking on the issue sooner and was worried that such sloppy work would cost him a contract. But when Helen Jones wrote back, she simply told him to revise the manuscript and change the title. Matt was thoroughly relieved and went ahead and made the changes, and resubmitted the manuscript.

Little, Brown once again liked what he had written, and Matt's third book, *Basketball Sparkplug*, was published in 1957. This book hit the hearts of many people. As a result, Matt won his first major award: The Boys Clubs of America Junior Award Certificate. Helen Jones sent the certificate along with this letter:

Dear Mr. Christopher:

I am sending you herewith the Certificate of Merit, awarded to you by the Boys Clubs of America for Basketball Sparkplug. *As Miss Vinton, Director of Publication Service for the Boys' Club, says in asking me to forward it to you, "We hope that he will be happy with it, as we are in giving it to him."*

Helen L. Jones

This nationwide recognition was just what Matt needed to spur him on. He was closer than ever to fulfilling his dream of writing full time — but he wasn't there yet. While some magazines were now paying up to a penny and a half to two cents a word, Matt still did not make enough income for him to quit his day job.

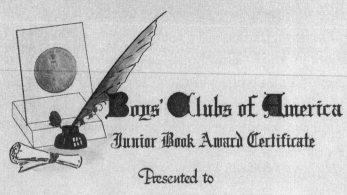

Boys' Clubs of America

Junior Book Award Certificate

Presented to

Matt Christopher

for The Book

Basketball Sparkplug

Selected as best liked by Boys' Club Members

April 11, 1958

Albert R. Cole
PRESIDENT

John M. Gleason
EXECUTIVE DIRECTOR

The Junior Book Award for *Basketball Sparkplug.*

Matt had returned to work at the National Cash Register (NCR) Company, having left GE when a promotion didn't come through. He spent his days at NCR handling orders from foreign companies. The job wasn't overly stimulating, but so long as Matt had his typewriter to turn to at night, he was satisfied.

Matt never got bored writing. He had so many interests that his topics were almost endless. He had always had a desire to fly airplanes, for example, and as a result, he did a tremendous amount of research in the field of aviation. Three of his stories about flying sold to three different magazines in 1957.

Matt also kept trying to market his second baseball manuscript, *No Baseball Allowed.* After numerous submittals, the Steck-Vaughn Company Publishers of Austin, Texas, bought the story. They asked for a few revisions and changed the title to *Slide, Danny Slide,* then published the book in 1958. That same year, Little, Brown published *Two Strikes on Johnny,* about a young baseball player and his blind brother.

With two books out in one year, Matt was hopeful that he was on the verge of a breakthrough with his writing career. He continued to turn out manuscripts, working almost simultaneously on *Little Lefty,* a baseball novel, and *Touchdown for Tommy*, which featured football. As always, he filled his books with plenty of sports action, realistic conflicts, and true-to-life feelings and experiences. He also tried to offer readers subtle messages about the importance of being a decent and caring human being.

Knowing how valuable Helen Jones's time was, he did his best to give her a glimpse of what his latest stories contained in the cover letters that accompanied the manuscripts.

"Dear Miss Jones," Matt's letter about *Touchdown for Tommy* read . . .

The story is about Tommy Fletcher, whose parents had died in an automobile accident, and who now lives in a foster home. Tommy's stay is indefinite. At anytime he may be taken away and given to another family for possible adoption.

Although his mother and father had given him a lot of love and devotion, Tommy had been brought up in a tough neighborhood. Thus, when Tommy mingles with the new boys and plays football with them, he is rough and doesn't play according to the rules. He does everything wrong. But the Powells have shown him such kindness that he has become attached to them, and wants to stay with them.

Tommy's trials and errors in trying to make the Powells keep him is the rest of the story.

I hope you like it.

Sincerely,
Matt Christopher

Helen Jones did like it. In fact, she accepted both *Touchdown for Tommy* and *Little Lefty*. As with *Basketball Sparkplug,* the realistic events of the books made them hits with young readers.

Having discovered what appealed to his audience, Matt made sure to sprinkle such events in his new manuscripts. Sometimes he used experiences from his own childhood as the basis for these events, but more and more he was finding that his present life as the father of four youngsters gave him plenty to work with.

In 1958 he was granted two weeks vacation from NCR. He and Cay thought it would be fun to travel through Canada and New England, camping along the way instead of staying in hotels. So they packed up Marty, Pam, Dale, and Duane in the 1953 Dodge, loaded the camping supplies, and started on their way.

The trip took the Christophers through the St. Lawrence River locks into Canada. The first night they camped on picnic grounds at the edge of a field. Cay, Matt, and Marty set the tent up — only their second time doing so — while the rest of the kids explored the surrounding area. That night, after a supper of sandwiches, they lit the kerosene lamp and talked until ten o'clock. By then, everyone was so tired they were ready to sleep.

Even though there were six people crammed inside a seven-foot tent, all were sleeping soundly until suddenly, a noise outside the tent jolted them awake.

Mooooooo!

Matt crawled outside — and froze. Not five feet away stood a Holstein bull. Matt and the bull stared at each other for a long moment. Then Matt said, "Scram, bull. Get out of here."

The bull did not move at first. Then, finally, it turned around and lumbered away, heading toward a clump of trees in the distance. Matt ducked back into the tent and reported that the coast was clear.

Cay believed him, but she wasn't in the mood to wait and see if the bull was going to come back. Even though it wasn't quite dawn, she got everybody up and told them to get their gear together. They rolled up the blankets, pulled up the stakes, hauled down the tent, stashed everything back into the trunk of the car, and headed north toward Quebec. That night they stayed in a hotel.

The memory of that heart-pounding confrontation stayed with Matt throughout the trip. When he got home, he used the incident as the basis for a scene in his next book, *Long Stretch at First Base*. Once again, his ability to create events that felt genuine earned him a contract with Little, Brown. The book, his sixth with the company, was published in 1960.

By this time Matt had written virtually every kind of story imaginable. Besides his children's books, he had published more than 200 short stories, articles, poems, and plays. Every one of them had its own special place in his heart.

Meanwhile, Matt Christopher's sports books were

finding a special place at Little, Brown. As sales of his titles increased, the publishing company realized that his novels were doing just what they'd hoped they would do: Fill a void in the children's book market. The name Matt Christopher was starting to be associated with good sports books for children, and Little, Brown made it clear that they wanted to continue publishing his manuscripts. By the early 1960s, he was receiving two to four new contracts a year; many of the contracts offered bigger advance payments and higher royalty percentages than the previous ones.

This ongoing relationship with Little, Brown finally allowed Matt to realize his lifelong dream of being a full-time writer. Thanks to the higher advances and the royalty income received from Little, Brown twice a year, the Christopher family was on solid financial footing. So on March 31, 1963, more than thirty years after he first dreamed of becoming a writer, he took the plunge. He retired from his job at NCR and began to write for a living.

Chapter Five:
1964–1973

A Man of Many Interests

Matt's dream might never have become a reality if not for the unfailing support of his family. Cay had always believed in her husband's talents and stood behind him completely when he made his decision to quit his day job. Marty, Pam, Dale, and Duane were all in school full time, but when they were home, they knew not to intrude when their father was working. And the children also provided something of great importance to Matt's writing: ideas.

Matt had been playing sports from the moment he was able to throw and catch a baseball, football, or basketball. He'd grown up in a time when many kids preferred playing sports to eating. Writing sports scenes was never a problem, but sometimes Matt needed inspiration for characters, conflicts, and themes. He often found that inspiration by focusing

The Christopher family in 1961. From left: Dale, Cay,
Matt, Marty, and Pam. Duane is in front of Matt.

on what was important to his children, their friends, and their families. He also looked back on his own life, delving into his own memories of childhood.

Matt had grown up eating, living, and breathing the concept of family values. The importance of love, respect, kindness, understanding, and togetherness was bred into him and were feelings he and Cay tried to instill in their children and into his books. Scenes of family dinners, of families attending church together, of helping one another with chores, of celebrating holidays and birthdays, or simply listening to each other's problems — all these and more happened in the Christopher household and in his books.

Matt knew that school was also a huge component in most children's lives. He had always regretted that he hadn't been able to go to college. He hoped his own children wouldn't have to feel that same regret. He made sure that they put their education first, before outside activities — and made sure his characters realized that school should come before sports.

Wingman on Ice, Matt's first hockey book, addressed this very issue. Tod Baker, the main character, isn't doing his best work. His teacher, Ms. Hudson, tries to steer him right:

"But you can't expect to review everything in one night and remember it all. Seems to me you're spending more time than necessary with something less important than your schoolwork. Education, you know, is more important than basketball."

"Hockey," he corrected her. "Not basketball."

Matt echoed Ms. Hudson's sentiments when he wrote an inscription in a copy of the book he gave to his son, Dale.

By 1965, Matt had added five more books to the Little, Brown list. That same year, three of his books were reprinted in paperback by Scholastic Book Services and offered to schoolchildren at a discount rate. The books were listed in flyers that were handed out during class. Whenever Matt's children received a flyer, they took great pride in showing their classmates the books their father had written. Local readers knew they had a celebrity in town — and it seemed that more and more children in other parts of the country knew to look under "C" when they wanted to read a good sports novel.

June 1, 1964

For Dale —

Congratulations on a successful baseball and track season, son.

But hit the books, too, for a good average! (Start with this one.)

Love

Dad

From Matt to his son, Dale.

But as fond as he was of writing sports stories, Matt began to yearn to return to the mystery genre. He approached Little, Brown and asked them if they'd be interested in publishing mysteries for children. They agreed to let him try his hand at them, but only if he published the books under a pseudonym. They were worried that his loyal readers might be confused otherwise. He settled on "Fredric Martin," a combination of his middle name and his confirmation name, and began to write.

As always, Matt reworked events from his own life and put them into his books. *Mystery on Crabapple Hill*, published in 1965, was based on the time his grandfather had been haunted in Portland Point all those years ago. His second title, *The Mystery Under Fugitive House*, featured a tavern in Lansing as the backdrop. The tavern was called the Rogue's Harbor Inn and had once been part of the Underground Railroad during the Civil War. The four-story brick building was built on a basement that had many secret compartments — the perfect setting, Matt thought, for a mystery.

Unfortunately, Frederic Martin's mystery books never saw the same strong sales of Matt Christopher's sports novels. After these two titles, Little, Brown chose not to publish any more. Matt was disappointed, for much as he loved writing sports novels, he was always eager to test his writing abilities and try something new. Still, he understood that publishing was a business that had to make money. And of course, he wanted to continue making money, too. So when Little, Brown encouraged him to write sports books, he happily complied. And as it turned out, he would soon be given a new opportunity that was completely different from anything he'd done before.

One morning in 1966, while ten-year-old Duane was at school and Cay was out doing errands, Matt got a call from the editor of *Treasure Chest Magazine.* Matt had sold a number of short stories to the publication, but still, having the editor contact him was unusual.

After a bit of chitchat, the editor got to the point of his call. He asked Matt if he was familiar with the *Chuck White* comic-strip series that had been published by *Treasure Chest Magazine* for the past twenty-five years. Matt said he was.

The editor explained that they were considering reworking the strip by creating a new Chuck White character. This character, also called Chuck White, would be the fourteen-year-old nephew of the old Chuck White. What they needed, the editor said, was someone to come up with new story lines for the strip. That someone had to know how to write for children. He believed the someone they were looking for was Matt Christopher.

Matt was excited. Here was his chance to break into new territory in his writing career. Even though he'd never written a comic strip in his life, he agreed to give it a try.

A couple of days later, he received a fat envelope in the mail from the George F. Pflaum Company in Dayton, Ohio, publishers of *Treasure Chest Magazine.* In the envelope were the last few episodes of the comic strip. Matt was to pick up the story line from these strips and continue it.

Matt read the strips then went right to work on an outline. Once he was satisfied with how the story unfolded, he wrote the script following the format the editor had mailed to him. After a couple of rewrites, he typed up the final copy, stuck it into an envelope with an accompanying letter, and mailed it.

Weeks passed. Waiting for a reply was agonizing,

and Matt was beginning to think that his script was a disaster. Then a letter came in the mail — not a rejected manuscript, but a note from *Treasure Chest Magazine's* editor who simply said, "Matt, you hit the bull's-eye! The script's great! Congratulations!" A contract for his services followed soon after.

Matt had tremendous fun writing the *Chuck White* series. He looked forward to receiving the comic-book proofs in the mail and seeing the drawings of *Chuck White* with the blank speech balloons coming out of the characters' mouths. It gave him great satisfaction to fill those balloons with words.

Matt now divided his time between writing scripts for *Treasure Chest* and sports novels for Little, Brown. But even a man as dedicated to his work as Matt needed to take a break every so often. In April 1967, he fulfilled his longtime desire of traveling to and from Europe by sea. Cay and Duane accompanied him on the SS *Breman* for a seven-day voyage across the Atlantic. They spent a few days in England visiting with Marty, who was stationed there with the U.S. Air Force, then crossed the English Channel and toured France, Germany, and Switzerland.

Even though he wasn't at his typewriter, Matt was

One of several *Chuck White* comics written by Matt.

still busy thinking of ideas to write about. While they were in Switzerland, he put together a story that he used as part of the *Chuck White* series. The plot sent Chuck White to Lucerne, Switzerland, in search of a treasure. Two "thugs" (as Matt called them) learn about the treasure and follow Chuck to Europe. The story line, a combination of a treasure hunt and good versus evil, was a success. And for the first time, Matt also had a hand in the strip's illustrations. He sent some of the photos he had taken in Switzerland to the magazine, which in turn sent them on to the artist. The results were amazing. The artist depicted the scenes of Switzerland just as it appeared in the pictures that Matt had sent to him.

The relationship between *Treasure Chest* and Matt Christopher lasted until 1973, when the magazine had to fold. Sales had dropped significantly due to competition from the growing number of paperback books available. Matt was brokenhearted. He had loved writing the series and was proud of the stories he had written.

But as it turned out, the story that was to become his bestselling book ever was just hitting its stride.

Chapter Six:
1973–1975

Home Runs — and a Few Strikes

During the years that he was writing the *Chuck White* series, Matt continued to send manuscripts to Little, Brown. His ideas and inspirations for stories seemed to be endless. All his books were centered around a sport, but they also highlighted life's true conflicts, such as divorce in the family, deaths in families, pressure to perform, disease, injury, coming into adolescence, and fears of the unknown. Every one of these concepts found its way into a Matt Christopher book.

Sometimes the stories were based on real events and people. *The Team That Couldn't Lose* featured a tough football coach who motivated his team to a perfect record. This character was drawn from Lansing Central High's own football coach, a local legend who had coached his team to four unbeaten seasons.

Some of his best stories, though, came straight from his imagination. Many contained an element of intrigue. And one, *The Kid Who Only Hit Homers,* introduced readers to a very mysterious man — Mr. George Baruth.

Matt, a longtime baseball player and fan, knew that hitting a home run was one of the greatest thrills ever for a player. It was also one of the most difficult things to do. The batter has to know how to stand, hold the bat, and move his arms and wrists. He has to have perfect timing to swing the bat just as the speeding baseball is coming at him. Matt had perfected all of these techniques during his short baseball career, but he didn't acquire this knowledge without the help of different coaches and teachers.

In *The Kid Who Only Hit Homers,* Sylvester Coddmyer III learns batting techniques that make him not just a good hitter, but a great hitter, one who could hit only home runs. Sylvester's teacher is Mr. George Baruth — a man most readers (but not Sylvester!) instantly recognized as being none other than George "Babe" Ruth.

Matt had great fun writing the tale of Sylvester and the mysterious Mr. Baruth and added a unique touch by including an author's note, something he rarely did in his books.

Author's Note

This story was told to the author by a person whose expressed wish is that he remain anonymous. Every word in it is true (so he said), except that names have been changed to protect the innocent (and those not so innocent).

The author was left to form his own opinion on whether the incidents have actually happened, and he prefers to keep that opinion to himself.

It is left to the judgment of the reader whether he wishes to do likewise.

Matt Christopher

Matt's author's note from *The Kid Who Only Hit Homers*.

Although readers knew that the story was made up, most were captivated by the idea that maybe, just maybe, a great ballplayer like the Babe might one day help them achieve greatness.

The publication of *The Kid Who Only Hit Homers* cemented Matt's place as the premier author of sports books for children. He was a mainstay on the Little, Brown list, his books almost sure purchases by libraries and a growing number of bookstores. Yet as content as Matt was with the way his career had developed, he once again yearned to try something different.

As usual, he looked to his own life for inspiration. Years earlier, when his children were still young, the family had owned three pets. Ginger, their first dog, was a mongrel, part collie and springer spaniel, and like most mongrels, she had a sunny disposition. She always appeared to be smiling and wagged her tail constantly. Besides Ginger, there was a dachshund named Winnie who belonged to Pam. Duane had a white Persian cat named Whitey.

In 1973, Matt convinced Little, Brown that he should write an adventure story about the two of Christopher's pets, Ginger and Whitey. *Desperate*

Search, about a misfortune that brings the two animals together, was a big departure for Matt, particularly because it was told from the perspective of Whitey the cat. Although the book was never as successful as his sports novels, Matt enjoyed the challenge of trying to think like a cat.

Matt followed up *Desperate Search* with another adventure novel titled *Earthquake!* This tale, set in the Adirondack mountains of New York, follows the plight of Jeff Belno and his horse, Red, after they're caught in an earthquake. Before writing the book, Matt did countless hours of research on the causes of earthquakes, especially the ones in New York State.

Matt's third and final adventure novel was *Stranded,* published in 1974. This book was born out of a truly thrilling adventure Matt and Cay had shared a year earlier.

Matt had always been interested in sailing. So when friends of theirs asked if they'd like to spend a few weeks living on a sailboat with them in the Caribbean, Matt jumped at the chance. Cay, too, was excited at the idea of sailing in such an exotic place. They both took sailing lessons on the lake near their home, and then they prepared for their journey.

The trip took them to Miami, Florida, then to Nassau, and finally to Georgetown in the Bahamas, where their thirty-foot sailboat, the *Mochica,* was moored. Loaded with enough food and ice for a week, Matt, Cay, and their friends motored out of Elizabeth Bay. They were given navigation charts to sail by and firm warnings about the many reefs and shallow waters. When they were in deep enough water, they hoisted the sails. Once under sail, Matt and Cay took their turns steering the ship. As soon as they got the feel of it, they didn't have any problem guiding the ship where they wanted it to go.

The voyage was everything they could have hoped for. They swam, sunbathed, and even snorkeled. It was during one snorkeling trip that Matt had a startling encounter.

Fitted with a mask, fins, and snorkel, Matt was admiring the beauty of the water surrounding him. Suddenly, something nudged him on the hip. He turned and came face to face with a long, slender fish. As the fish stared at him with enormous eyes and worked its jaws and gills, Matt realized just how unprotected he was in the water. IIis heart started pounding.

A minute or two passed, then the fish made a slow U-turn and calmly swam away. Matt got out of the water as fast he could. Even after he learned that the fish was a barracuda — and not a shark as he'd feared — it took him some time to calm down.

The rest of the trip went smoothly except for one near catastrophe. Despite their accurate charts, they ran the ship aground on a bed of sand. They were stuck for what seemed like forever, searching in vain for other ships to help them. Luckiliy, as twilight grew near, the tide changed, and the *Mochica* made its way clear.

These adventures in the Bahamas did not go untold. After their return to upstate New York, Matt used his encounters with the barracuda and the near stranding in his third and final adventure story, *Stranded,* about a blind boy named Andy Crossett and his dog, Max, who are left high and dry on an island in the tropics after a storm.

With *Stranded,* Matt felt that he had finally put together a real winner, with a convincing story and a real problem for the main character. The plot had a lot of action, and Andy and his dog had many obstacles to overcome. But when *Stranded* was published in 1974, it met with little success.

Matt tried to take the failure of his non-sports books in stride, stating his belief that "few authors are blessed with a talent such that everything they write sells. In the long run, then, it is the persevering person who sticks with it, through thick and thin, that reaches the top rung of the writing ladder."

And when all was said and done, he still had a faithful and ever-increasing audience for his sports books. In fact, many children who had read his books were now adults, some with children of their own. These adults were doing what many parents do, sharing their favorite authors with their children. Matt Christopher books were about to reach a whole new generation of readers.

Chapter Seven:
1976–1997

The #1 Sportswriter for Kids

In 1976, thirteen years after Matt had become a successful full-time author, he and Cay made one of the biggest moves in their lives. The winters of upstate New York were taking their toll on the couple. After many long talks, they decided to leave the snow and slush behind and move to Venice, Florida. Matt and Cay were sad to leave their children and grandchildren behind, but both looked forward to enjoying warm, sunny weather year-round.

Venice was a true paradise, and Matt and Cay soon settled into an agreeable routine. Matt wrote in the mornings, then went for a swim. In the afternoons, he and Cay were busy visiting with friends, taking day trips to interesting places in the state, or accepting invitations to go sailing. Even after long days, many nights found Matt back at his typewriter.

A lot had changed in the sporting world since the sale of *The Lucky Baseball Bat* in 1954. Little, Brown was quick to inform Matt that to keep his books fresh and appealing, he needed to keep up with kids' sports interests. So more and more, Matt was exploring sports other than baseball, football, and basketball.

Matt had never thought that America's pastime, baseball, would take a backseat to any sport. But in the late 1970s, soccer was becoming the most popular sport for all ages. Matt knew the rudiments of soccer, but in order to write about it, he had to know the sport inside and out. His hard work paid off. In 1978 *Soccer Halfback* was published and quickly became one of his bestselling titles.

A year later, he broke new ground again with *Dirt Bike Racer,* followed by *Drag Strip Racer* and *Dirt Bike Runaway.* All three books were set in Florida and featured troubled youths in search of stability.

Meanwhile, Cay was in search of stability of a different sort. Ever since moving to Florida, she had been troubled by the yearly reports of destructive hurricanes. She believed it was only a matter of time before their home was hit — and that was not something she felt neither she nor Matt was prepared for.

103

Matt, center, with glasses, is surrounded by his wife,
children, and grandchildren in 1996.

Then their son Duane, now a landscape architect living in Rock Hill, South Carolina, recommended that they move to his town. The weather wasn't as warm as it was in Florida, but they would be a lot closer to their children and grandchildren. And they would be out of the path of future hurricanes. The idea sounded good to Matt and Cay, so in 1983 they moved to Rock Hill.

Cay made friends easily and soon became active in the community and the church. Matt settled into a routine of writing and working in the yard. He also took time to remodel their three-bedroom house into a one-bedroom with a large study.

This study became the home of Matt's first computer. His eldest grandson, Chris, encouraged him to buy a word processor, and when Matt finally agreed, Chris's father, Chuck, found him one. Matt didn't sleep a wink the next few nights, worrying that he was too old to operate it. But his grandson reassured him. "It's easier than you think, Grandpa, and once you learn how to operate it, you'll wonder why you had never bought one before."

Matt did get used to the word processor and later, his first desktop computer. But he didn't forget how anxious he had been. He channeled all that emotion into his first sports novel for girls.

In the early 1980s girls were playing more organized sports, especially softball. Matt chose this sport for his novel and in 1985 published *Supercharged Infield*. Writing from a girl's perspective was difficult, but Matt had never been one to shy away from a challenge. He sprinkled the tale with lots of softball action and gave the story an aura of science fiction. In the long run, girls who read the book never seemed bothered by the fact that it was written by a man in his late sixties. They just enjoyed the story.

Supercharged Infield was the seventy-second Matt Christopher book published by Little, Brown since 1954. Many of his titles were now available in paperback as well as hardcover. Because paperbacks are less expensive than hardcover editions, bookstores were more willing to shelve them because they knew they would sell. Employees at these same bookstores knew just where to direct customers in search of a good sports book for children — to the Matt Christopher shelf.

The eighties were a very busy time for Matt. He added a few more girls' sports stories to his list and also started writing books for younger readers. He put together a series of books about a sports-loving dog called Harry that had extrasensory perception, or ESP. Matt also wrote *Return of the Home Run Kid,* a sequel to his bestselling book *The Kid Who Only Hit Homers.* Before this book was published, if anyone asked Matt what his favorite title was, he would answer, "I don't have one. It is like asking me which one of your kids do you like the best." But he liked *Return of the Home Run Kid* so much that it became his all-time favorite.

During this same time, two of Matt's books were nominated for awards. In 1989, *Dirt Bike Racer* was nominated for the Maud Hart Lovelace Award, given to the author whose children's book is judged best in the state of Minnesota. Matt was thrilled that a book he'd written ten years earlier was included in the list of nominees. In 1992, Massachusetts Best Children's Book Award nominated *Spy on Third Base.*

Neither book won an award, but in the following year, Matt was honored by the children of Atlanta, Georgia. They had voted him to be the recipient of the Milner Award, given to their favorite author. Matt was very touched by the award and flew down to

Atlanta to give a speech. Giving speeches was not his strongest suit, but he knew the children were counting on him. He didn't want to disappoint.

Matt Christopher had now been writing and publishing children's books for nearly four decades. Somewhere along the way, he had become famous. For some people, fame happens at one single event, but not for Matt. Becoming famous started when he was that little boy selling magazines and telling himself that he wanted to become a writer.

Matt had become a bestselling author the only way he knew how: through hard work and dedication to his craft. And through all the trials and tribulations of his struggling career and into his years of success, he remained true to himself. He took life one day at a time, and he learned from his mistakes. He made sure his wife, his children, and his grandchildren knew how much they meant to him. His warmth and kindness overshadowed many misfortunes. He never said anything unkind about anyone. He believed everyone always had some good in them.

Matt often said that he would not know what he would have done if he hadn't been bitten by the writing bug. He could not have been happy doing anything else. He would always thank God for giving him the ability to put down on paper what he enjoyed in real life and enlarge it by using his imagination to its fullest.

Matt Christopher lived by a simple philosophy: "Don't ever stop doing what you believe. Don't ever let anyone stop you from realizing your dream."

Epilogue

In February 1983, Matt had a frightening experience. He lost control of his equilibrium and collapsed against the casing of a door in his house. The doctor who examined him couldn't find anything wrong, but did warn that it could happen again.

It did, two years later. Examinations and CT scans provided no answers.

A few years later Matt was overcome with nausea. Darkness overwhelmed him. Cay quickly got him to emergency room service, and again they took a CT scan. This time, they discovered a tumor of the pituitary gland. In January 1985, Matt underwent brain surgery to remove the growth.

The surgery appeared to be a success, and as days passed Matt got stronger. Then, six months later, he

The hero of Rock Hill, South Carolina — and
everywhere else his books are known!

suffered a relapse. Tests revealed that there was a regrowth of the tumor.

Matt and Cay traveled to Boston, Massachusetts, where he was given radiotherapy at the Massachusetts General Hospital. These treatments were administered every day for weeks at a time. They left Matt weak and disoriented, but in the end, they seemed to have worked.

Matt continued to live his life and do all the things that he loved to do — to write and putter around the house. In the spring of 1997, he was given a Hero's Award by the city of Rock Hill.

But in the summer of that same year, the tumor returned. Matt had his third operation to remove it. He fought the illness with everything he had, but this time it was just too much for him. On September 20, 1997, he passed away in Charlotte, North Carolina.

Matt Christopher left behind a legacy of books and generations of grateful readers. Today his family works hard to keep that legacy alive, to ensure that children born in the years after Matt's death can enjoy the many books he so loved writing.

Matt and Cay.

Names were changed to Christopher after arrival to USA, 1904

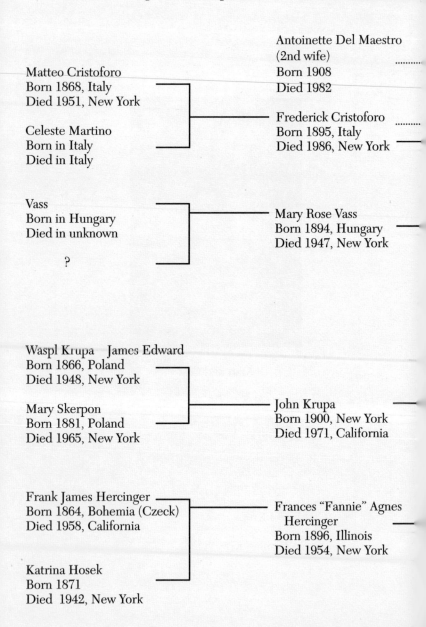

Antoinette Del Maestro
(2nd wife)
Born 1908
Died 1982 ....

Matteo Cristoforo
Born 1868, Italy
Died 1951, New York

Celeste Martino
Born in Italy
Died in Italy

Frederick Cristoforo ....
Born 1895, Italy
Died 1986, New York ——

Vass
Born in Hungary
Died in unknown

?

Mary Rose Vass
Born 1894, Hungary
Died 1947, New York ——

Waspl Krupa   James Edward
Born 1866, Poland
Died 1948, New York

Mary Skerpon
Born 1881, Poland
Died 1965, New York

John Krupa ——
Born 1900, New York
Died 1971, California

Frank James Hercinger
Born 1864, Bohemia (Czeck)
Died 1958, California

Katrina Hosek
Born 1871
Died 1942, New York

Frances "Fannie" Agnes
  Hercinger ——
Born 1896, Illinois
Died 1954, New York

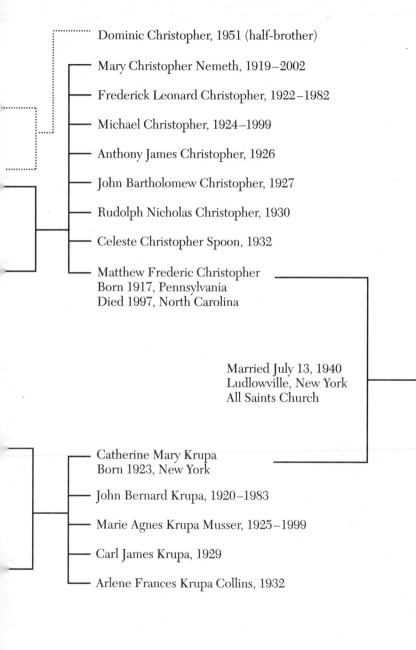

Dominic Christopher, 1951 (half-brother)

Mary Christopher Nemeth, 1919–2002

Frederick Leonard Christopher, 1922–1982

Michael Christopher, 1924–1999

Anthony James Christopher, 1926

John Bartholomew Christopher, 1927

Rudolph Nicholas Christopher, 1930

Celeste Christopher Spoon, 1932

Matthew Frederic Christopher
Born 1917, Pennsylvania
Died 1997, North Carolina

Married July 13, 1940
Ludlowville, New York
All Saints Church

Catherine Mary Krupa
Born 1923, New York

John Bernard Krupa, 1920–1983

Marie Agnes Krupa Musser, 1925–1999

Carl James Krupa, 1929

Arlene Frances Krupa Collins, 1932

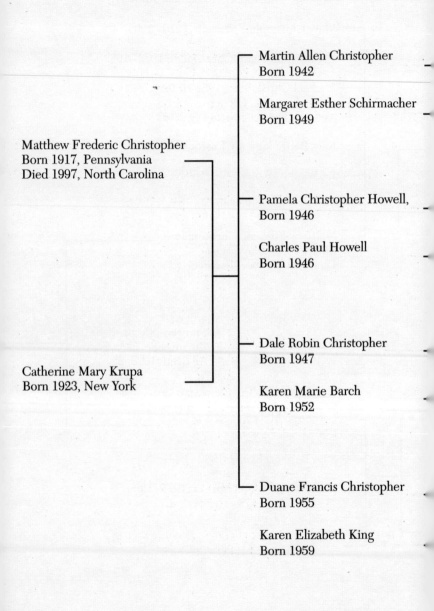

Martin Allen Christopher
Born 1942

Margaret Esther Schirmacher
Born 1949

Matthew Frederic Christopher
Born 1917, Pennsylvania
Died 1997, North Carolina

Pamela Christopher Howell,
Born 1946

Charles Paul Howell
Born 1946

Dale Robin Christopher
Born 1947

Catherine Mary Krupa
Born 1923, New York

Karen Marie Barch
Born 1952

Duane Francis Christopher
Born 1955

Karen Elizabeth King
Born 1959

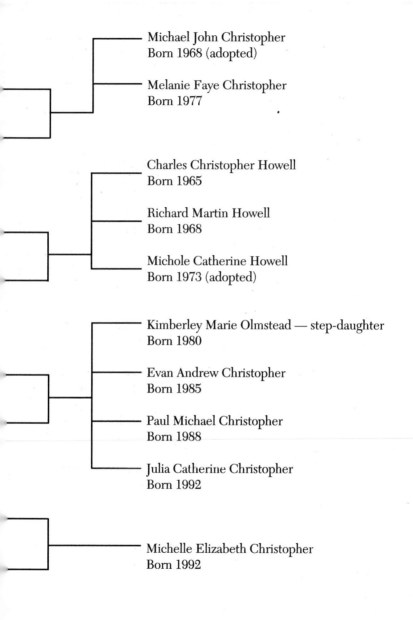

Michael John Christopher
Born 1968 (adopted)

Melanie Faye Christopher
Born 1977

Charles Christopher Howell
Born 1965

Richard Martin Howell
Born 1968

Michole Catherine Howell
Born 1973 (adopted)

Kimberley Marie Olmstead — step-daughter
Born 1980

Evan Andrew Christopher
Born 1985

Paul Michael Christopher
Born 1988

Julia Catherine Christopher
Born 1992

Michelle Elizabeth Christopher
Born 1992

The #1
Sports Series
for Kids

Read them all!

*Originally published as *Crackerjack Halfback*

All available in paperback from Little, Brown and Company

Matt Christopher®

Lance Armstrong

Kobe Bryant

Jennifer Capriati

Terrell Davis

Julie Foudy

Jeff Gordon

Wayne Gretzky

Ken Griffey Jr.

Mia Hamm

Tony Hawk

Grant Hill

Ichiro

Derek Jeter

Randy Johnson

Michael Jordan

Mario Lemieux

Tara Lipinski

Mark McGwire

Greg Maddux

Hakeem Olajuwon

Shaquille O'Neal

Alex Rodriguez

Curt Schilling

Briana Scurry

Sammy Sosa

Venus and
Serena Williams

Tiger Woods

Steve Young

SOCCER 'CATS